LIVING WITH
DEAFNESS

Emma Haughton

RAINTREE
STECK-VAUGHN
PUBLISHERS
A Steck-Vaughn Company

Austin, Texas

Titles in the series

Living with Asthma

Living with Blindness

Living with Cerebral Palsy

Living with Deafness

Living with Diabetes

Living with Down Syndrome

Living with Epilepsy

Living with Leukemia

Published by Raintree Steck-Vaughn Publishers, an imprint of Steck-Vaughn Company

Library of Congress Cataloging-in-Publication Data
Haughton, Emma.
Living with deafness / Emma Haughton.
    p.   cm.—(Living with)
    Includes bibliographical references and index.
    Summary: Explains the condition of deafness, its possible causes, and how it affects the everyday lives of those who are dealing with it..
    ISBN 0-8172-5742-X
    1. Deafness—Juvenile literature.
    2. Deaf—Juvenile literature.
    [1. Deaf.. 2. Physically handicapped.]
    I. Title. II. Title: Deafness
RF291.37.H38   1999
617.8—dc21   98-32231

Printed in Italy. Bound in the United States.
1 2 3 4 5 6 7 8 9 0 03 02 01 00 99

Picture acknowledgments
The publishers would like to thank: John Birdsall 11 (top), 17, 27; Eye Ubiquitous/Paul Seheult 24; Sally and Richard Greenhill *cover* (bottom) 7, 25, 26; Science Photo Library/Bo Veisland, MI&I 6, /Simon Fraser (Brompton Day Hospital, Cumbria) 7; Trip/S. Grant 19; Wayland Picture Library 16, /Angus Blackburn *cover* (main), 28, /Martin F. Chillmaid title page, 4–5, 8, 9, 12–15, 18, 21–3, 29, 31, /Tim Woodcock *cover* (top); Zefa 11 (bottom), /Ed Bock 10. Special thanks to Barbara Shalit for all her work on this book.

Contents

Meet Tom, Gita, Alison, and Alfred

Tom, Gita, Alison, and Alfred look the same as everyone else, although they are all deaf. Unless someone wears a hearing aid or uses sign language, you can't always tell if the person is deaf.

Like many other young children, Tom had a blockage in his ears caused by fluid. When he was little, Tom had trouble keeping up with classes at school because it was difficult for him to hear his teachers.

▷ Gita is determined that her deafness will not keep her from enjoying life.

Gita goes to the same school as her hearing brothers, even though she hears very little because she once had a condition called meningitis. By wearing a hearing aid and by speech-reading, Gita manages well at school. She has many hearing friends.

◁ Tom has a lot of friends, but sometimes he finds it difficult to hear what they are saying.

4

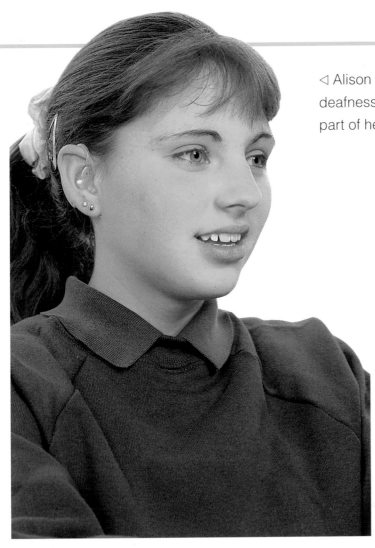

◁ Alison accepts her
deafness as a normal
part of her life.

Alfred could hear very well when
he was young. However, working
in a noisy factory for many years
has resulted in deafness. As Alfred
grew older, he could hear less and
less. His doctor has suggested that
Alfred could wear a hearing aid to
help him hear better, but Alfred is
not sure if he wants to wear one.

Alison was born profoundly deaf. She hears
very little, even when she wears a powerful
hearing aid. She has never heard her own
voice, and her speech is not as clear as that
of her hearing friends. Even though Alison
can talk and speech-read, she prefers to
communicate with her deaf friends at
school by using sign language, a system
based on hand and arm movements,
gestures, and facial expressions.

▷ Alfred finds it difficult
to accept his deafness.

What is deafness?

Deafness means a hearing loss so severe that even with a hearing aid, a person cannot hear spoken language. People who are hard of hearing can understand speech if they use a hearing aid.

Our ears enable us to detect a range of different sounds as well as speech, and our brain allows us to make sense of the sounds we hear. When sound waves enter the brain, they travel through the ear canal and cause the eardrum and the ossicles in the middle ear to vibrate. When these vibrations reach the inner ear, they stimulate the thousands of hair cells in the cochlea. The hair cells send an electrical message to the brain telling us what we hear.

▽ The ear is a complex and delicate part of the body.

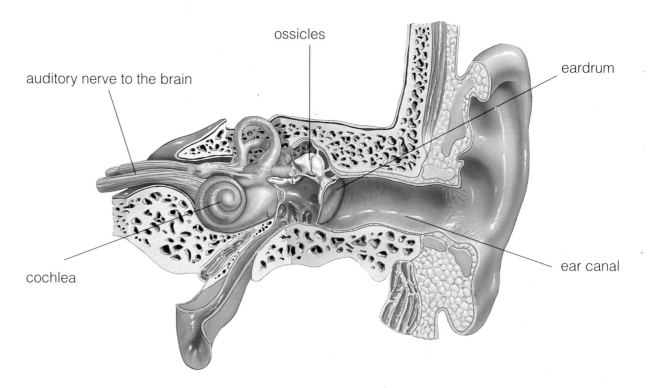

ossicles

auditory nerve to the brain

eardrum

cochlea

ear canal

▷ Many people need to use a hearing aid as they grow older.

There are different levels of hearing loss. Some people can hear loud sounds but not very quiet sounds. Some people can hear sounds that are low in pitch but not those that are high-pitched. Very few people have no hearing.

There are many reasons why some people have difficulty hearing. Some people are born with hearing problems because their mother had rubella, or measles, during pregnancy. Hearing loss can also be caused by persistent loud noise, fluid in the ear, or an infection.

◁ In some cases, particularly when a child is born deaf, no one knows the reason.

Aids to hearing

Technology can help most deaf children and adults. Many deaf people wear hearing aids to help them hear better. Very few people are completely deaf. Sometimes a hearing aid can boost the amount of sound they can hear, though it can never restore hearing completely. The most common hearing aids are worn behind the ear. They are carefully chosen to match the amount and type of hearing loss of their user. Some hearing aids that fit right into the ear are very small and hard to see.

▽ Gita is so used to her hearing aid that she rarely notices she is wearing it.

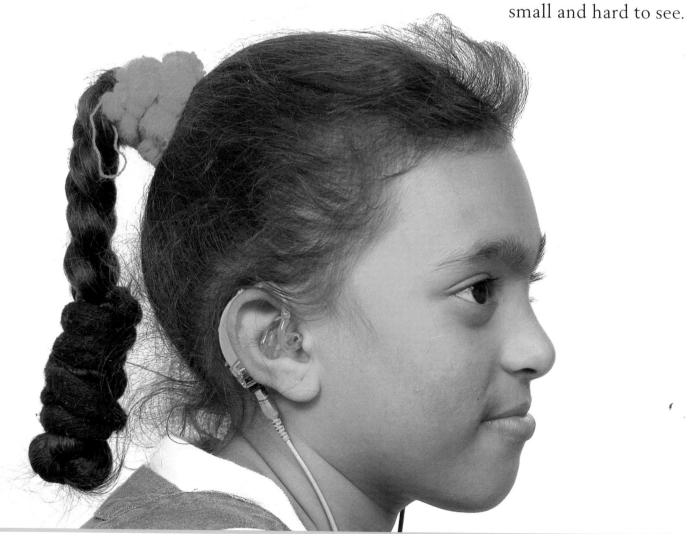

△ Like many deaf people, Tom often watches people's lips to understand what they are saying.

Cochlear implants can improve hearing for some deaf people. The implants are surgically placed in the inner ear, in the cochlea. A small microphone, worn behind the ear, picks up sound and transmits it to the inner ear. From there, the sound waves continue into the brain.

Some types of hearing loss may be temporary and disappear when a child grows. However, deafness has many different causes, and not all are easily managed. Many countries use vaccinations to help prevent diseases, such as mumps, measles, and meningitis, that can sometimes cause deafness in children.

Aids to communication

Modern technology can be a big help for deaf people at home and at work. The Internet, for example, lets you talk to someone by typing into a computer rather than using a telephone. Closed captioning allows deaf people to read what people are saying on television programs.

Deaf people can now use the telephone more easily, with devices that make conversation louder or services that show what hearing people are saying as words on a screen. Deaf people can also talk to each other over a TTY, which is a special phone that allows you to type in messages and then read them on screen.

▽ Deaf people can use computers to communicate with someone instead of using a telephone.

△ TTYs help deaf people communicate by using the telephone.

◁ In the future, videophones may allow people to communicate by speech-reading and using sign language.

Noisy public places, such as shopping malls and railroad stations, can be difficult for people wearing hearing aids. There are devices that can help. Induction loops cut out background noise and allow deaf people to tune in to announcements and information through their hearing aids. Other devices, such as vibrating or flashing alarms and bells, can warn of risks like fire.

Not all aids for deaf people rely on technology. Many people communicate by writing notes. Hearing dogs can help deaf people in much the same way as guide dogs aid blind people, by alerting their owners to possible dangers. For deaf people who use sign language, a sign language interpreter is often the most important aid to communication.

Growing up with deafness

When Tom's hearing was tested as a baby, he did not seem to be deaf. But Tom's parents noticed that as he grew older, Tom was slow to talk and often didn't seem to hear what people said. At school, Tom's teacher noticed he was having trouble with his work and with speaking and listening in class.

▽ Tom's doctor detected his hearing problem by looking into his ears.

Being careful

"I can hear clearly now, but I still have to be careful. When I go swimming, I have to keep my ears out of the water, which is sometimes difficult."

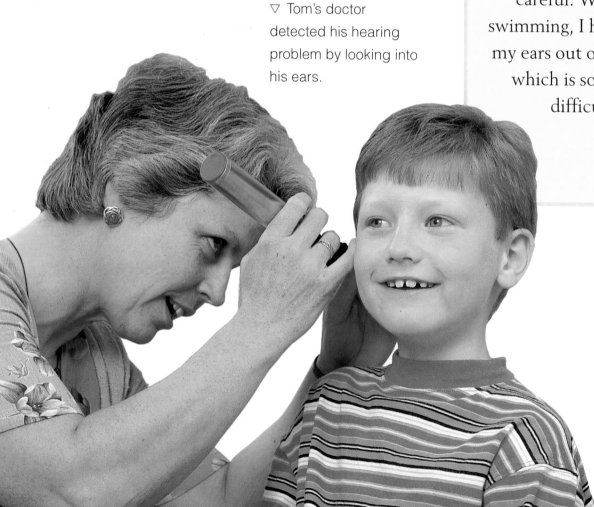

△ Tom finds it easier to talk to his friends in quiet places where he can hear them more clearly.

The family doctor examined Tom's ears and found that he had a thick fluid in his ears that kept him from hearing properly. The doctor explained it was like trying to hear through water. She said that the problem would go away, but Tom's hearing seemed to get worse. Another doctor decided that Tom needed an operation. Small plastic tubes were put into his ears to help drain away the fluid. Tom can now hear very well, but he has to be careful not to get water in his ears.

Some children who have more serious hearing losses, or who are born deaf, develop their communication skills over several years, often at a school for deaf children. Tom's hearing problems were mild and lasted only a few years. He did not find it too hard to catch up with his speech and schoolwork.

Learning to communicate

When Alison was a baby, her parents noticed that she didn't seem to hear most sounds. After some tests, her doctor discovered that she was profoundly deaf. A teacher of deaf children came to the family's house and showed Alison's parents how to help her learn to communicate.

◁ Alison's communication skills developed well at her school.

Alison went to a school for deaf children when she was five years old. Although at home she had learned to understand a lot of what people were saying just by speech-reading, she found it very difficult to talk clearly herself. At school, Alison learned to speak more clearly. Being in a school with a lot of other deaf children also helped her develop sign language.

Using sign language

![colour swatch bar]

"My deaf friends and I prefer to use sign language to communicate with each other. It's easier to express your feelings and more relaxing than using speech."

△ For Alison, gesture and sign language have always been the ways that she prefers to communicate.

Now that Alison is a teenager, she understands a lot of what people say to her, and her speech is quite clear. But Alison still finds speech-reading and talking very tiring, especially for long periods. Sign language has always been easiest for her.

A deaf person in the family

◁ Sometimes parents worry about the safety of their deaf child crossing the street or going to the corner store alone. Their parents might not allow their deaf child to do things that their hearing children do regularly.

Although some deaf children also have deaf parents, brothers, or sisters, most deaf children are born into families where everyone else can hear. This situation can be difficult for parents because they may need to learn new ways to communicate with their deaf child.

Being a deaf child in a hearing family can sometimes feel a bit lonely. You can feel left out of conversations that are going on around you. It is harder to join in games with your brothers and sisters if you find it difficult to understand what they are saying.

It can be hard for hearing children in the family, too. They may feel that their deaf brother or sister seems to get more attention from their parents, or they may get angry that their parents often expect them to help their deaf brother or sister. If the deaf child in your family doesn't use sign language or if you find it difficult to learn how to sign, sometimes it can be frustrating trying to understand each other.

▽ Families often learn sign language to help communicate with a deaf family member.

Most families, however, learn ways to cope with these difficulties, and most deaf children can grow up feeling as much a part of the family as anyone else.

Going to school

Most deaf children go to their neighborhood schools with their hearing friends. Some can use hearing aids, but others, like Gita, use an FM system combined with hearing aids to help them listen to what their teachers are saying. With an FM system, a teacher wears a microphone that transmits his words, using radio waves.

Some deaf children also use an interpreter. An interpreter is a person who translates what the teacher is saying into sign language. Teachers trained in teaching deaf children may also help out in the classroom.

△ Gita's teacher wears a microphone that directs what he is saying straight to her hearing aid.

Some children, like Alison, go to schools where all the students are deaf. These schools have teachers who are specially trained to teach the deaf and to help them develop good reading and writing skills. Schools for the deaf teach all the same classes as a regular school does. It may take some deaf children a long time to learn to read because their sign language is different from English. This means that they have to work very hard to keep up in reading and writing. Schools for the deaf also have speech therapists who work with students to improve their speech and their listening and speech-reading skills.

▽ With special help, deaf children can learn very quickly.

Attitudes toward the deaf

Gita enjoys going to the same school as her hearing brothers and has many hearing friends. When she first started at the school, she was the only deaf child there.

Although she loves making new friends, Gita doesn't always like the way people treat her. Sometimes they ignore her and talk to her parents and brothers instead. Sometimes they speak very slowly or shout into her hearing aid, which hurts her ears. This can make Gita feel very angry and upset.

△ Gita's friends aren't bothered about her deafness.

Wearing a hearing aid

"At first, I found it hard when other children stared and asked me about my hearing aid, but now no one seems to notice."

Gita finds it easier to communicate well if people talk to her in a quiet place and look straight at her so she can speech-read easily. It also helps if they gesture and use facial expressions. Gita understands most of what people say, but if she doesn't understand something, she needs to ask people to say it again. When she does get things wrong, it helps if people keep calm and say the same thing again in a slightly different way.

▽ Gita finds it easier to communicate with people if they look at her directly when they talk.

Missing sound

△ Alfred misses hearing the birds singing in his garden.

Alfred was not always deaf, but working for years in a noisy job and old age have gradually resulted in his hearing loss. Alfred finds his deafness very hard to accept. Unlike Alison, who has always been deaf, Alfred can remember quite clearly what it was like to hear well. It upsets him that he can no longer listen to his favorite music.

Alfred's doctor has suggested that he should wear a hearing aid, but Alfred has put it off for many years. Much of the time he prefers to think that his hearing is not really so bad. But Alfred is finding his deafness more and more difficult to manage. He finds it harder to understand what people are saying and once was nearly hit by a speeding car that he couldn't hear approaching. Unlike Alison, he has not developed other skills such as speech-reading to help him manage.

Those of us who hear well often take our ability for granted. It is easy to forget how much we rely on our hearing to help us in our daily lives.

Doctor's advice

"My doctor thinks I should wear a hearing aid. I've thought about it many times, and I've finally decided it is probably time to get a hearing aid."

Deaf people at work

Deaf people work in almost every occupational field. There are deaf doctors, dentists, carpenters, engineers, and teachers. There are deaf people working in business, the clergy, nursing, teaching, counseling, and television production. Deaf people can drive and hold noncommercial pilot's licenses, and they enjoy sports and hobbies like everyone else.

▽ Companies often find it useful to have deaf staff who can communicate with deaf customers.

In 1990 The Americans with Disabilities Act opened the workplace to people with disabilities, including deaf people. Now, because of ADA, companies provide technology and services to help deaf people participate in the workplace alongside all other Americans.

In many countries the government encourages employers to employ and support deaf people. Many employers provide TTYs and flashing fire alarms for their deaf employees. Some companies provide sign language meetings so deaf people can follow what people are saying. Some employers also provide training courses to help their hearing staff improve their communication skills with deaf people so that deaf and hearing people can work together more effectively.

△ Deaf people can do most jobs as well as their hearing colleagues.

The ADA and technological advances have helped many deaf people overcome practical difficulties in the workplace. Today, problems often result from the wrong attitudes and expectations of hearing people. Many people wrongly assume that deaf people cannot do good jobs and therefore do not give them a chance to try.

The deaf world

espite TTYs, faxes, writing notes, and using interpreters, communication with the hearing world often presents problems for deaf people. Deaf people often just feel more comfortable with one another. They can understand one another better than they can understand hearing people. They communicate easily by using sign language.

▽ Clubs for deaf children can be a chance to improve sign language skills.

△ Deaf clubs offer a chance to meet other deaf people.

In many places, there is a deaf culture and community that hearing people are often not even aware of. On the Internet, for example, there are a lot of sites for deaf issues and information.

You could almost say that deaf people are part of a huge worldwide club. Sharing many interests and experiences in life, deaf people of different nationalities often have much more in common than hearing people of different nationalities. Although deafness can be a barrier with hearing people, for many deaf people in a hearing society, it is also a bond.

Getting help

Most countries have organizations that can offer assistance to deaf people and their families. Regular hearing checks help doctors find deaf babies and children early, so that their parents can get the support they need to adapt to their child's deafness.

◁ Sometimes it is much easier to share your problems and worries with other people who have been through similar experiences.

There are also many organizations that provide advice, support, and information about everything from medical services to technological developments. They can bring deaf people and their families together so they can talk and support one another.

There are many organizations that provide information, support, and services for deaf people in the United States. Here are some you might like to call or write:

Alexander Graham Bell Association for the Deaf
3417 Volta Place NW
Washington, DC 20007-2778
(202) 337-5220, V/TTY
http://www.agbell.org

American Society for Deaf Children
1820 Tribute Road, Suite A
Sacramento, CA 95815
(800) 942-ASDC (parent hot line)
(916) 641-6084 (business, voice, TTY)
http://deafchildren.org

National Association of the Deaf
814 Thayer Avenue
Silver Spring, MD 20910-4500
(301) 587-1788, V
(301) 587-1789, TTY
(301) 587-1971, FAX

Glossary

Closed captioning On screens, it tells what characters are saying and describes music and background sounds.

Cochlea Part of the inner ear that helps conduct sound.

Communication The ways in which people keep in touch and pass on ideas and feelings to others.

Ear tubes Small plastic tubes that are placed in the ear.

Fluid Something that is not solid, such as water.

FM unit A device that receives sounds spoken into a microphone and transmits them to a hearing aid.

Gesture Movement of the body to express something.

Hearing aid Small device worn behind or inside the ear that can increase hearing. Hearing aids are carefully chosen and programmed to match the amount and type of hearing loss of their user.

Induction loops A sound system within a building that enables deaf people to hear announcements through signals transmitted to their hearing aids.

Infrared audio enhancement A sound system used in theaters and movie theaters that receives sound signals through infrared light beams.

Interpreter Someone who changes one language to another.

Microphone A small device that picks up sound.

Profoundly deaf When someone is profoundly deaf, he or she hears very little.

Sign language A communication system using hands and body in different positions to express thoughts, feelings, and ideas.

Speech therapist Someone who can help others learn to improve their speaking, listening, and language skills.

Speech-read To know what someone is saying by watching the shapes their lips make when they speak, their face, and their gestures.

TTY A special phone that allows people to speak to each other by typing messages rather than speaking.

Vaccination An injection that can help prevent someone from catching a disease.

Videophone Telephone system that uses pictures as well as sounds.

Further information

Colleges and Universities
Gallaudet University
800 Florida Avenue NE
Washington, DC 20002-3695
(202) 651-5000
http://www.gallaudet.edu

National Institute for the Deaf
Rochester Institute of Technology
1 Lomb Memorial Drive
Rochester, NY 14623
(716) 475-2411
http://www.rit.edu/considering/prospectus/colleges/ntid.html

Magazines
HIP Magazine
http://www.hipmag.org
An award-winning, nonprofit publication for today's deaf and hard of hearing children.

Deaf Life
http://www.silentnews.org
"The deaf community's #1 magazine." Written and produced by deaf people for the deaf and hearing communities.

Web Sites
Deaf World Web
http://dww.deafworldweb.org
"The Central Deaf Point on the Internet." The largest and leading deaf web site, providing a comprehensive deaf-related resource on the Internet. Information includes news stories, discussion forums, resources, research, products and services for sale, deaf kids and youth section, penpals, art and talk groups.

Index

Numbers in **bold** refer to pictures as well as text.